Avalynn's
COLORING BOOK

Avalynn's Coloring Book
© 2023 by Ashton Bohannon

Written by Ashton Bohannon
Illustrated by Nadia Ronquillo

ISBN: 9-7-982-181995-2-4

Prologue

The way that people perceive themselves is central to everything in life. If Gods people will visualize themselves as children of a holy and powerful God, then they will walk according to that calling and position. Gods children are not like the devils children. Gods children are unlike the rest of the world.

When the Bible is read and rightly divided it is evident that Jesus gave His people power and authority. He expects us to walk boldly as warriors in His kingdom. He wants us to succeed and prosper in life.

We are sinners UNTIL we join into Gods family. Once we say yes to Jesus, we become heirs and partakers of a royal and divine nature. When we say yes to Jesus, we become a new creation and an heir to His throne. Gods people do not have to tolerate the enemy or his kingdom, because Gods kingdom rules and reigns over all forever and ever Amen.

But as many as received Him, to them He gave the right to become children of God, to those who believe in His name who were born, not of blood, nor of the will of the flesh, or of the will of man, but of God. John 1 12

Therefore if any man be in Christ, he is a new creature old things are passed away behold, all things have become new.   2 Corinthians 5 17

Joshua 1 8. This Book of the Law shall not depart from your mouth, but you shall meditate on it day and night, so that you may be careful to do according to all that is written in it. For then you will make your way prosperous, and then you will have good success.

The scriptures within this book have been taken from The New King James Bible and The New Living Translation Bible.

Colossians 1:16
For by Him all things were created that are
in heaven and that are on the earth, visible
and invisible, whether thrones or dominions or
principalities or powers. All things were created
through Him and for Him.

Proverbs 24: 3-4
Through wisdom a house is built, and
by understanding it is established;
By knowledge the rooms are filled with
all precious and pleasant riches.

Ezekiel 36: 26-27

I will give you a new heart and put a new spirit within you; I will take your heart of stone and give you a heart of flesh. I will put My Spirit within you and cause you to walk in My statues, and you will keep My judgments and do them.

Luke 10:19

Behold, I give you the authority to trample on serpents and scorpions, and over all the power of the enemy, and nothing shall by any means hurt you.

Psalm 103:19

The Lord has established His throne in heaven,
And His kingdom rules over all.

John 10:27-30

My sheep hear My voice, and I know them, and they follow Me. And I give them eternal life, and they shall never perish; neither shall anyone snatch them out of My hand. My Father who has given them to Me, is greater than all; and no one is able to snatch them out of My Father's hand. I and My Father are one.

Matthew 16:27
For the Son of Man will come in the glory of His Father with His angels, and then
He will reward each one according to his works.

Ephesians 6:10-11
Be strong in the Lord and in the power of His might. Put on the whole armor of God, that you may be able to stand against the schemes of the devil.

Walk with Avalynn through the maze as she finds her way to Jesus.

James 1:25

But he who looks into the perfect law of liberty and continues in it, and is not a forgetful hearer but a doer of the work, this one will be blessed in what he does.

Mark 11: 23-24

For assuredly, I say to you, whoever says to this mountain, 'Be removed and be cast into the sea,' and does not doubt in his heart, but believes that those things he says will be done, he will have whatever he says. Therefore, I say to you, whatever things you ask when you pray, believe that you receive them, and you will have them.

1 John 5:14
Now this is the confidence that we have in Him,
that if we ask anything according to His will,
He hears us. And if we know that He hears us,
whatever we ask, we know that we have received
what we have asked of Him.

Mark 16:17-18

And these signs will follow those who believe: In My name they will cast out demons; they will speak with new tongues; they will take up serpents; and if they drink anything deadly it will by no means hurt them; they will lay hands on the sick and they shall recover.

Proverbs 28:1

The wicked flee when no one pursues them,
But the righteous are bold as a lion.

John 15:7-8
If you remain in Me and My words remain in you, ask whatever you wish, and it will be done for you. This is to my Father's glory, that you bear much fruit, showing yourselves to be my disciples.

Acts 2:38

Repent, and let every one of you be baptized in the
name of Jesus Christ for the remission of your sins;
and you shall receive the gift of the Holy Spirit.

Matthew 13:23

But the seed falling on good soil refers to someone who hears the word and understands it. This is the one who produces a crop, yielding a hundred, sixty or thirty times what was sown.

Matthew 7:24-25

Therefore whoever hears these sayings of Mine, and does them, I will liken him to a wise man who built his house on the rock: and the rain descended, the floods came, and the winds blew and beat on that house; and it did not fall, for it was founded on the rock.

1 John 5:4-5
For everyone who has been born of God overcomes the world. And this is the victory that has overcome the world- our faith. Who is it that overcomes the world except the one who believes that Jesus is the Son of God?

Ephesians 2:6

And God raised us up with Christ and seated us with Him in the heavenly realms in Christ Jesus.